HOW TO DRAW BIRDS

Bald eagle

Mark Bergin

BOOK HOUSE

Published in Great Britain in MMXIV by
Book House, an imprint of
The Salariya Book Company Ltd
25 Marlborough Place, Brighton BN1 1UB
www.salariya.com

ISBN: 978-1-909645-53-0

SCRIBO   BOOK HOUSE   SCRIBBLERS

3 5 7 9 8 6 4 2

A CIP catalogue record for this book is available from the British Library.

Printed and bound in China.

Reprinted in MMXX.

Author: **Mark Bergin** was born in Hastings in 1961. He studied at Eastbourne College of Art and has specialised in historical reconstructions as well as aviation and maritime subjects since 1983.

Editor: Jacqueline Ford

Visit
www.salariya.com
for our online catalogue and
free fun stuff.

PAPER FROM

SUSTAINABLE
FORESTS

Contents

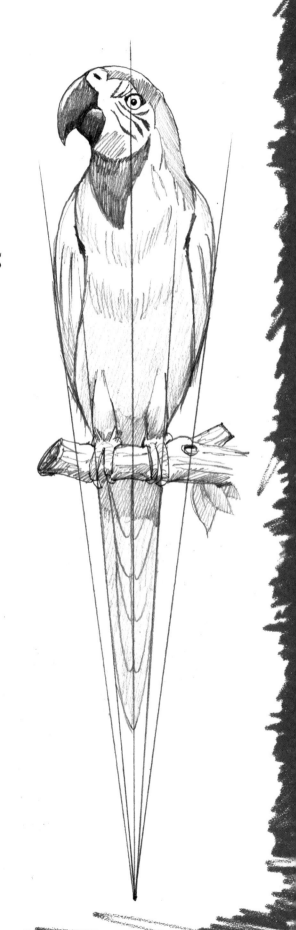

Making a start

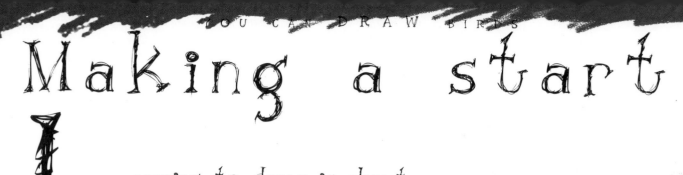

Learning to draw is about looking and seeing. Keep practising and get to know your subject. Use a sketchbook to make quick drawings. Start by doodling, and experiment with shapes and patterns. There are many ways to draw; this book shows only some of them. Visit aviaries and natural history museums, look at artists' drawings, see how friends draw, but above all, find your own way.

Drawing from models may be helpful.

These quick sketches begin with simple ovals.

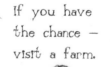

If you have the chance — visit a farm.

Use photos to capture birds in motion.

Good artists keep a sketchbook handy at all times.

Practice makes perfect. If your first attempt doesn't look right, don't be afraid to start again.

Using photos

Drawing from photographs is a useful way to study the shape of a bird as it moves. It's much easier than trying to draw a bird in flight!

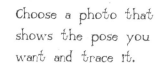

Choose a photo that shows the pose you want and trace it.

Draw a grid of equal-sized squares over the traced photo. This divides the image into small sections.

Light source

Lightly mark out a grid of the same proportions on your drawing paper. You can enlarge or reduce the size of an image by drawing larger or smaller squares. Now copy your original tracing, square by square.

In the drawing above, the arrow labelled 'light source' shows which direction light is coming from. Those parts of the bird that face away from the light source are in shadow so add shading to make your drawing look three-dimensional.

Add a background to complete the scene and to create an interesting picture. Don't forget to shade in the trees and house.

7

Perspective

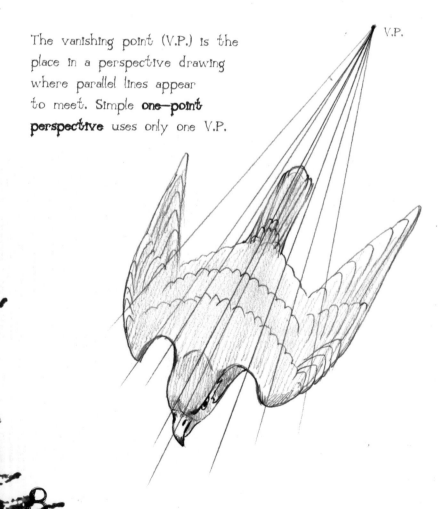

If you look at any object from different viewpoints, you will see that the parts that are closest to you look larger, and the parts that are further away look smaller. Perspective drawing helps to create a feeling of depth. It is a way of suggesting three dimensions even though you're drawing on a flat surface.

The vanishing point (V.P.) is the place in a perspective drawing where parallel lines appear to meet. Simple **one-point perspective** uses only one V.P.

V.P.

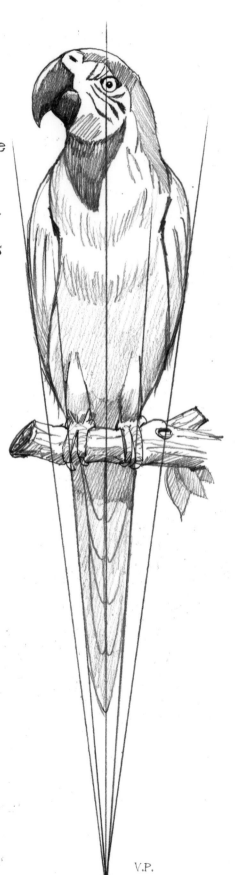

V.P.

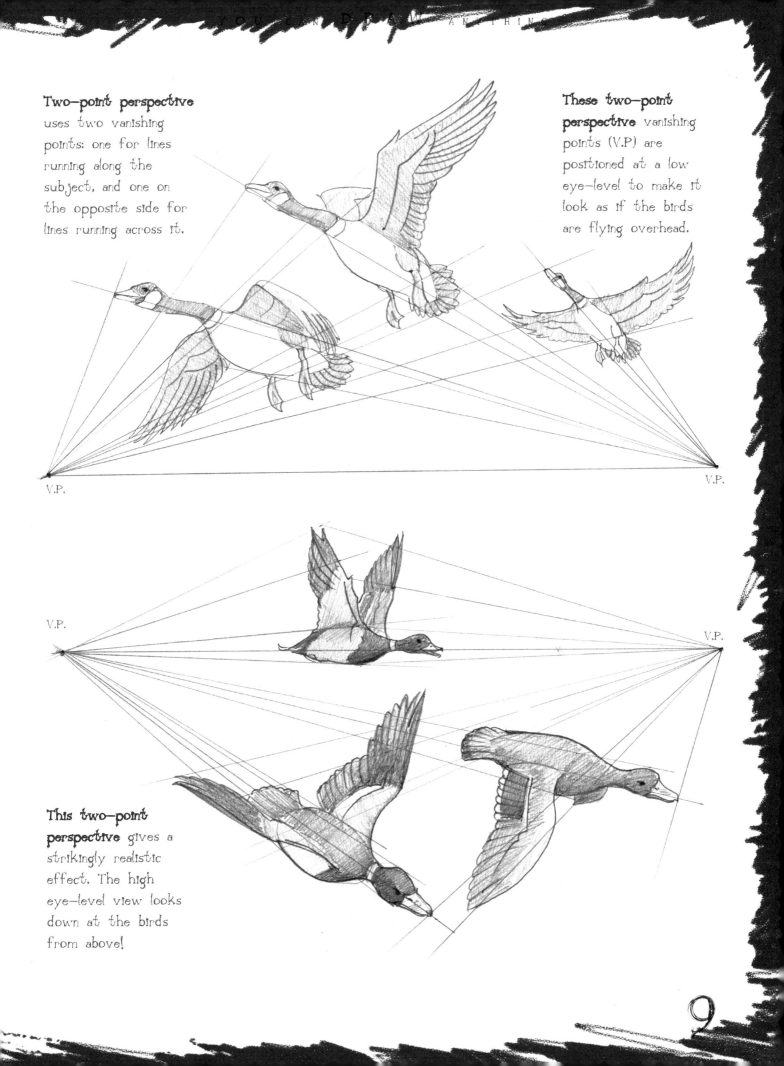

Two-point perspective uses two vanishing points: one for lines running along the subject, and one on the opposite side for lines running across it.

These two-point perspective vanishing points (V.P) are positioned at a low eye-level to make it look as if the birds are flying overhead.

V.P.

V.P.

V.P.

V.P.

This two-point perspective gives a strikingly realistic effect. The high eye-level view looks down at the birds from above!

9

Drawing materials

Try using different types of drawing paper and materials. Experiment with charcoal, wax, colouring pencils, crayons and pastels. All pens, from felt-tips to ballpoints, will make interesting marks — you could also try drawing with pen and ink on wet paper.

Hummingbird: colouring pencils

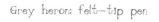

Grey heron: felt-tip pen

Colouring pencils and felt-tip pens are simple to use, and experimenting with them will result in drawings that are vibrant and intriguing.

Artist's tip:
Be careful: lines drawn with a felt-tip pen cannot be erased! Take your time.

Ink drawings cannot be erased, so keep your ink drawings sketchy and less rigid. Don't worry about mistakes as those lines can be hidden in the drawing as it develops.

Toucan: fineliner ink pen

Silhouette is a style of drawing that shows only a solid black shape, like a shadow.

Osprey and salmon: ink silhouette

Song thrush: pencil

Hard **pencils** are greyer and soft pencils are blacker. Hard pencils usually range from 6H (the hardest) to 5H, 4H, 3H, 2H and H. Soft pencils are graded from B, 2B, 3B, 4B and 5B up to 6B (the softest). HB is betweeen H and B.

11

Feet, wings and beaks

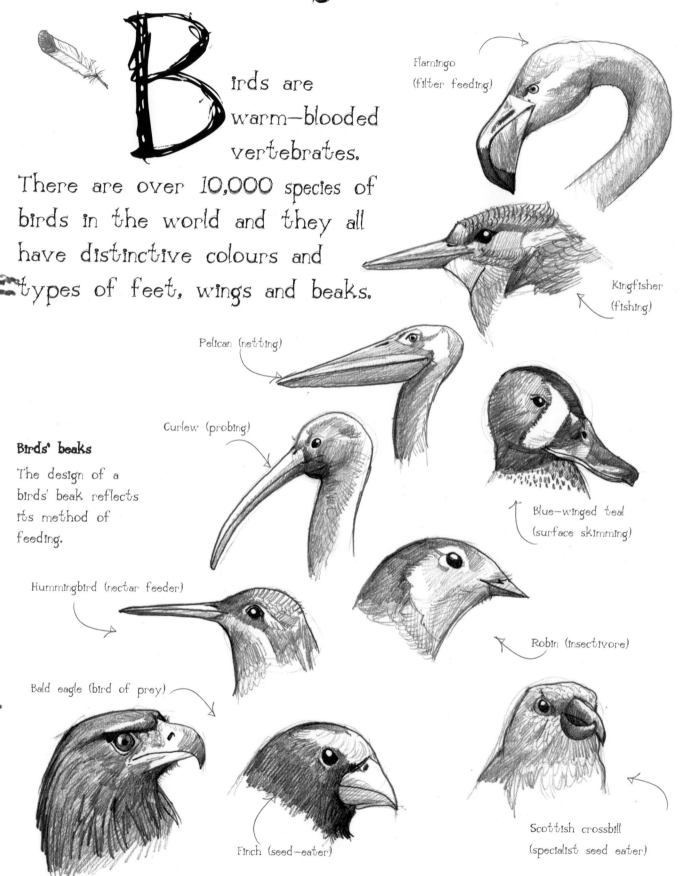

Birds are warm—blooded vertebrates. There are over 10,000 species of birds in the world and they all have distinctive colours and types of feet, wings and beaks.

Birds' beaks

The design of a birds' beak reflects its method of feeding.

Flamingo (filter feeding)

Kingfisher (fishing)

Pelican (netting)

Curlew (probing)

Blue—winged teal (surface skimming)

Hummingbird (nectar feeder)

Robin (insectivore)

Bald eagle (bird of prey)

Finch (seed—eater)

Scottish crossbill (specialist seed eater)

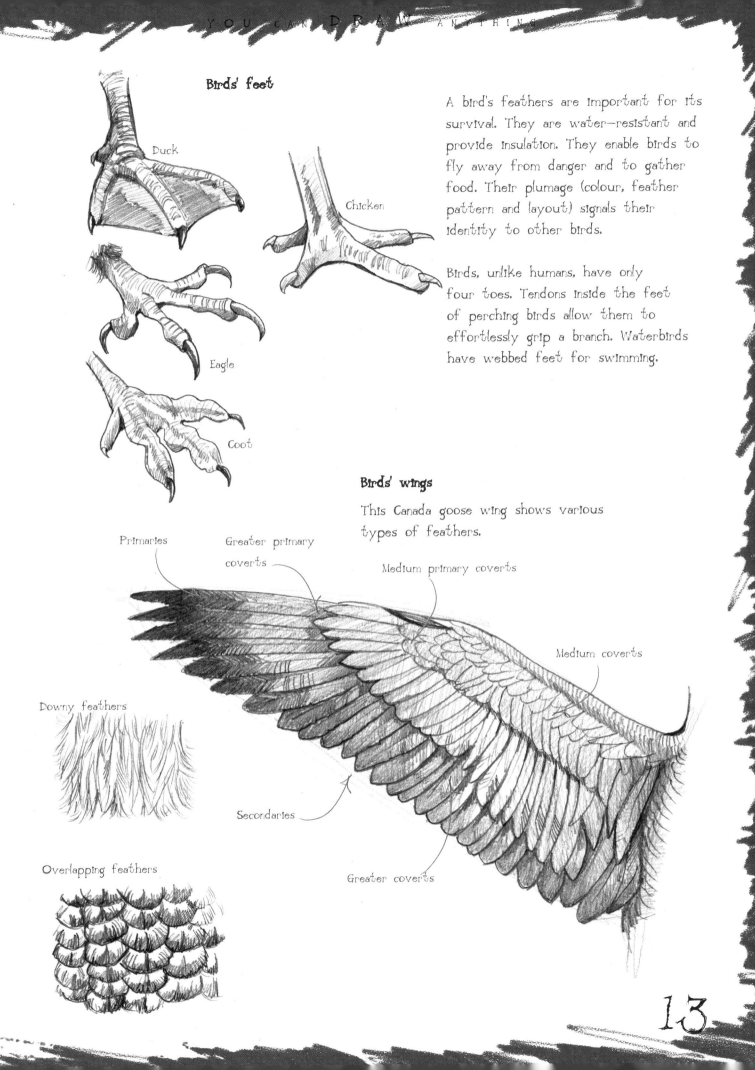

Birds' feet

Duck

Chicken

Eagle

Coot

A bird's feathers are important for its survival. They are water—resistant and provide insulation. They enable birds to fly away from danger and to gather food. Their plumage (colour, feather pattern and layout) signals their identity to other birds.

Birds, unlike humans, have only four toes. Tendons inside the feet of perching birds allow them to effortlessly grip a branch. Waterbirds have webbed feet for swimming.

Birds' wings

This Canada goose wing shows various types of feathers.

Primaries

Greater primary coverts

Medium primary coverts

Medium coverts

Downy feathers

Secondaries

Greater coverts

Overlapping feathers

13

Birds in flight

Birds rely on their ability to fly for survival. They remain airborne by flapping their wings and can choose to glide, swoop, change direction or hover.

Diving

Gliding

Hovering

Starting to dive

Swallow in flight

Quick sketches like these can capture the distinctive
shapes made by different birds in flight.

Mute swan

Mute swans are the heaviest flying birds. Their name derives from the fact that they make less sound than other swans.

Lightly draw in two oval shapes for the head and body.

Head

Body

Add curved lines for the neck to join the head and the body.

Neck

Tail

Draw in the pointed tail using two curved lines.

Take particular care with the head details. Use shading and careful pencil drawing to get the swan's eyes and beak right.

Draw in the legs and feet underneath the body.

Sketch in the shape of the webbed feet.

16

Start adding details to the head by drawing in the beak and the eyes.

Sketch in the shape of the wings.

Start to add form by shading areas of definition on the body and neck.

Note that one wing looks narrower than the other because the swan's body is turned at an angle.

Shade in those parts of the swan that face away from the light source.

The feet need to be shaded much darker. Add a ground line to complete the drawing.

Begin to add feathers to the wings. Draw in jagged lines to create the tail feathers. Then add shading.

Remove any unwanted construction lines.

17

Duck and ducklings

Head

Body

Ducks dive under the water to feed. A male duck is known as a drake whereas a female duck is called a hen. Duckling is the name of a baby duck.

Lightly draw two oval shapes to create the head and the body.

Add curved lines for the neck and to form the pointed tail.

Neck

Tail

Start adding details to the head by drawing in the beak and the eye.

Male mallard duck

Draw in the duck's legs and feet. The toes are webbed for swimming.

Start drawing the wing structure with an oval shape within the body. Add curved lines that meet at a point to complete the wing.

Add the tail feathers.

Use straight lines, dots and overlapping scale-shapes to represent the bird's feathers. Now add shading.

Female mallard duck and ducklings

Complete the duck by shading its body according to the direction of the light source.

Finally, bring your drawing to life by adding ducklings, water, a rock and long grasses.

Remove any unwanted construction lines.

19

Chickens

Chickens are estimated to outnumber all other bird species. They are domestic birds.

Start by drawing two oval shapes for the head and the body.

Head

Body

Tail

Neck

Add curved lines for the neck. Now draw in the tail using two curved lines that meet at a point.

Comb

The chicken's head is shown in profile. Pay attention to the position of both the beak and comb.

Draw in the chicken's legs, one behind the other. The toes form sharp talons.

Draw a curved line across the middle of the body for the wing. Form the comb and the tail using zigzag lines. Draw in the wing feathers with softer curves.

Wattle

Draw in the fleshy part surrounding the eye. Add the wattle.

Add shading. Leave white areas for the lightest parts.

Draw in the feathers using small, overlapping curved lines. Add skin texture to the legs and feet.

Add the darkest areas of tone to areas furthest from the light source and also to define shape.

Remove any unwanted construction lines.

21

Herring gulls

Herring gulls are large birds. They can grow up to 66cm in length. They are usually seen near coasts and around rubbish dumps.

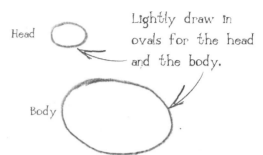

Head

Body

Lightly draw in ovals for the head and the body.

Draw in curved lines for the neck. Sketch in basic shapes for the wing and tail.

Draw the beak and eyes. Add feathers to the wings.

Draw the legs and webbed feet underneath the body.

Composition

Composition is the arrangement of a picture on the paper. See if your drawing looks better in an upright ('portrait') rectangle, or a horizontal ('landscape') rectangle.

Add shading to areas where light would not reach.

Draw in a post for the gull to stand on.

Remove any unwanted construction lines.

Head   Body

Draw a circular shape
for the head and a
long oval for the body.

Draw in the eye and beak.
Add curved lines to connect
the head and body. Draw
a rectangular shape for
the tail.

Draw the wing shapes using
curved lines. Add lines for
the tail feathers and draw
in the feet.

Add feathers to the
wings. Curve the end
of each line.

Add shading to the
areas where light
would not reach.

Add heavy tone for
the dark wing tips.

Remove any unwanted
construction lines.

Try drawing the
gull in other poses.

23

Barn owl

Barn owls prey on mice and other small rodents. They are nocturnal creatures.

Head

Body

Draw two overlapping ovals for the head and body.

Draw curved lines to join the head and body.

Sketch in the blunt-ended tail.

Draw in the owl's legs and feet. Add a large talon to each toe.

Negative space
Look at the shapes left between the lines of your drawing. This can help you spot mistakes.

Draw a v shape at the top of the head to define the face.

Start drawing the owl's wing using curved lines

Draw in the eyes and beak.

Draw in the owl's prey, caught in its talons.

Now draw in sections of the owl's wing. Use straight lines to add long feathers to the lower part of the wing.

Finish off the face and add pattern detail to the wings.

Add tone. Use directional strokes to create the appearance of small feathers.

Remove any unwanted construction lines.

Kingfisher

Kingfishers are vibrantly coloured birds. They have large heads, sharp bills (beaks) and tiny feet. They hover above water before diving in to catch underwater creatures.

Draw two overlapping ovals to create the head and body.

Head

Body

Link the head to the body using curved lines.

Add a triangular shape to create the tail.

Sketch in the shape of the kingfisher's feet and a branch to perch on.

Draw in a long
pointed beak.

Add an eye.
Draw in sections
of plumage on
the head.

Draw in a wing. Add a
series of curved lines
for the feathers.

Add more detail
to the branch.

Add short lines to
create the striped
head markings.

Use directional lines
to add tone to
suggest feathers.

Add shading to
areas where light
would not reach.

Using a mirror
Look at your drawing in a
mirror. Seeing it in reverse is
like looking at it through a
fresh pair of eyes — it can
help you to spot mistakes.

Add detail to complete
the branch.

Remove any
unwanted
construction lines.

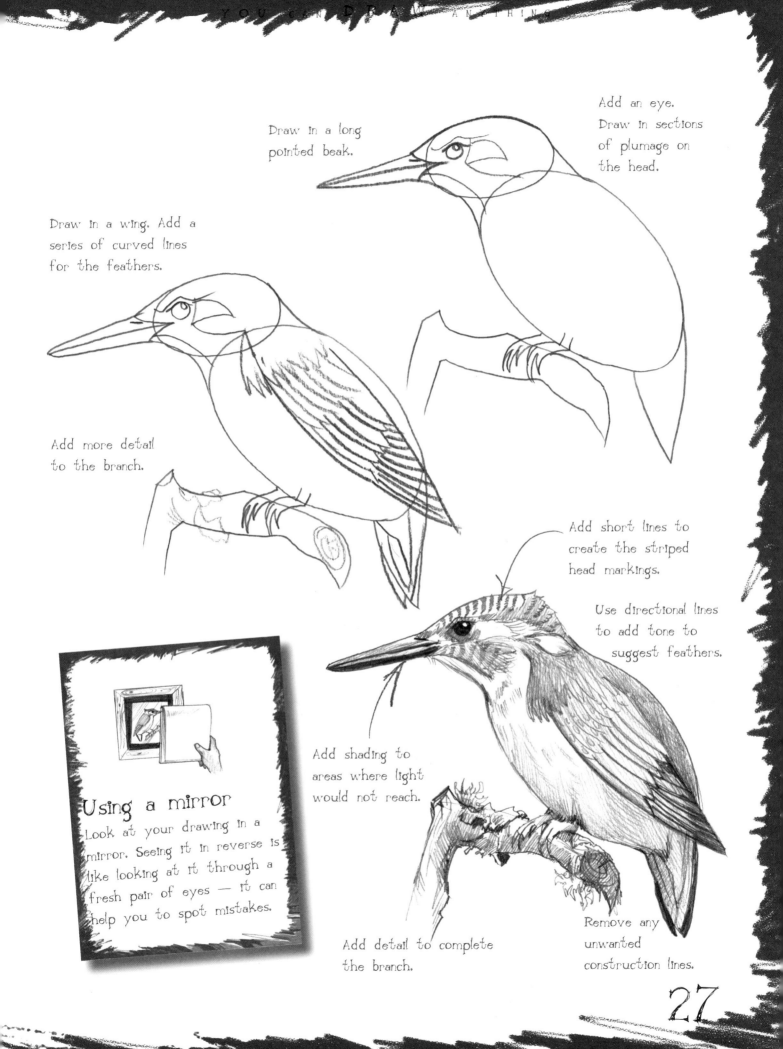

27

Robin

The European robin, shown here, is smaller than the American robin. Robins are always associated with Christmas. They lay pale blue eggs.

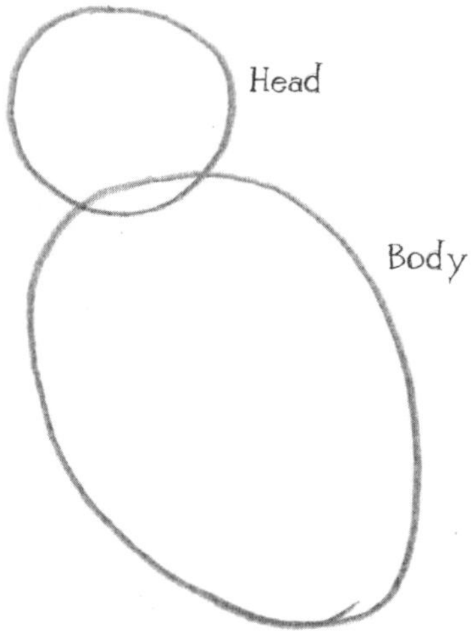

Head

Body

Draw two overlapping oval shapes for the head and the body.

Use curved lines to connect the head and body.

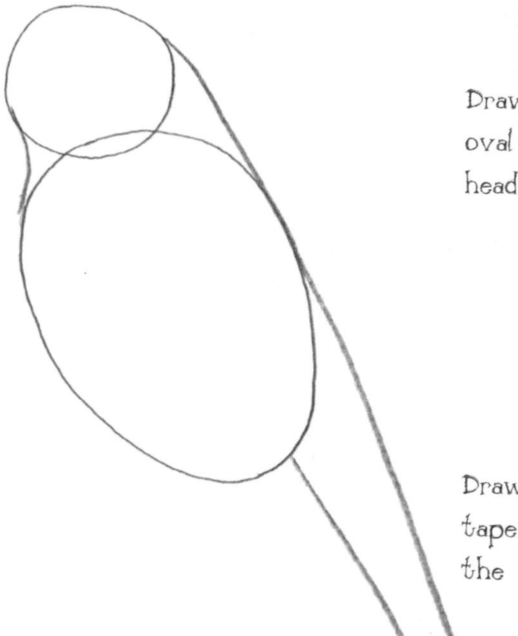

Draw a long, tapering shape for the tail.

Sketch in the position of the robin's feet.

Draw in a small, sharp beak.

Draw in one eye and the outline for the face and breast.

Add a dark line behind the eye.

Rougly sketch in the shape of the branch.

Draw in the robin's wing. Use long lines to delineate the feathers.

Add more detail to the branch.

Add dark tone to define the wings.

Add tone to the robin's face and breast.

Draw in the feet grasping the branch.

Add shade to areas light would not reach.

Remove any unwanted construction lines.

Bald eagle

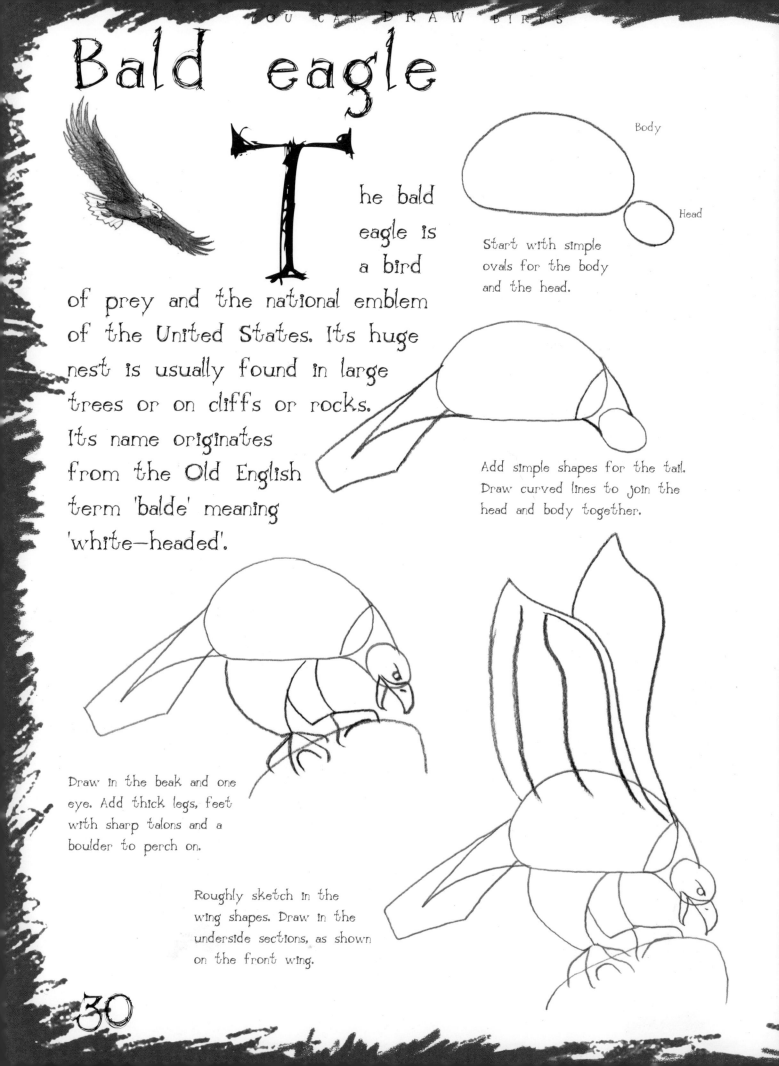

The bald eagle is a bird of prey and the national emblem of the United States. Its huge nest is usually found in large trees or on cliffs or rocks. Its name originates from the Old English term 'balde' meaning 'white-headed'.

Body

Head

Start with simple ovals for the body and the head.

Add simple shapes for the tail. Draw curved lines to join the head and body together.

Draw in the beak and one eye. Add thick legs, feet with sharp talons and a boulder to perch on.

Roughly sketch in the wing shapes. Draw in the underside sections, as shown on the front wing.